Trans Global:

Transgender then, now and around the world

Honor Head

FRANKLIN WATTS
LONDON • SYDNEY

First published in 2018
by Franklin Watts

Copyright © Franklin Watts 2018

All rights reserved.

Editor: Sarah Peutrill
Series designer: John Christopher
Picture researcher: Diana Morris

ISBN 978 1 4451 6048 1

Printed in Malaysia

Franklin Watts
An imprint of
Hachette Children's Group
Part of The Watts Publishing Group
Carmelite House
50 Victoria Embankment
London EC4Y 0DZ

An Hachette UK company.
www.hachette.co.uk
www.franklinwatts.co.uk.

The website addresses (URLs) included in this book were valid at
the time of going to press. However, it is possible that contents
or addresses may have changed since the publication of this
book. No responsibility for any such changes can be accepted
by either the author or the Publisher.

Every effort has been made to accurately depict the stories of
the people in the book and to trace the copyright owners of
the images. If any errors or omissions have occurred this is
unintended and will be corrected in future editions of the book.

With thanks to IntersexUK for their help.

Picture credits: AJP/Shutterstock: 16tl. AP/REX/
Shutterstock: 18, 56. Courtesy of aravaniartproject.
com:17t. In association with "The Dawgz"; 17b. In
association with St+Art India. Bettmann/Getty Images:
35. J. Bicking/Shutterstock: 7. Paul Brown/Alamy: 49.
Jonathan Browning/REX/Shutterstock: 44. Jean Catuffe/
Getty Images: 37. Courtesy of Bridget Clinch: 39.
Creatista/Shutterstock: 11b. CRS Photo/Shutterstock:
11cl, 14, 16tr. Earlyspatz/CC. Wikimedia Commons: 46t.
Focus on Sport/Getty Images: 36. Fotoholica Press/Getty
Images: 50b. Fox Photos/Getty Images: 29. Zack Frank/
Shutterstock: 11cr. Geartooth Productions/Shutterstock:
11tr. Horizons WWP/TRVL/Alamy: 6t, 24, 25. Georg
Kristiansen/Alamy: 22. Teresa Kroeger/Getty Images:
8. llewellynchin/Shutterstock: 11tl. Douglas Miller/Getty
Images: 31. Mark Miller/CC Wikimedia Commons: 23.
Michael Molony/Shutterstock: 9. Indranil Mukherjee/AFP/
Getty Images: 15. Museum of New Mexico: 12. New York
Daily News Archive/Getty Images: 34. Courtesy of Lydia
Nibley, Producer/director TWO SPIRITS: 13. 916 Collection/
Alamy: 27. PD/Publicity Photo: 33. PD/Wikimedia
Commons: 26, 28t, 28b from The Life and Adventures
of James P. Beckwourth, 1856.lev radin/Shutterstock:
45, 54, 55. reddees/Shutterstock: 16b. Courtesy of
Luisa Revilla: 50t. Jill Richardson/Shutterstock: 58.
Eddy Risch/EPA/REX/Shutterstock: 42. Miguel Rojo/
AFP/Getty Images: 51. rorem/Shutterstock: 40. Gabriela
Sanchez/AP/Rex/Shutterstock: 4b. Sipa Press/REX/
Shutterstock: 43tr, 43b. SOPA Images Ltd/Alamy: 21t, 21b.
Justin Starr Photography/Shutterstock: 5. Stephanie/
REX/Shutterstock: 43tl. Eduardo Verdugo/AP/REX/
Shutterstock: 19t, 19b. Wellcome Images/CC Wikimedia
Commons: 30. WENN Ltd/Alamy: 10, 46b. Xinhua/Alamy:
52. ZUMA/Alamy: 20tl, 20tr.

Every attempt has been made to clear copyright. Should
there be any inadvertent omission please apply to the
publisher for rectification.

The use of pronouns
We have used the pronouns of the preferred gender of the person
concerned. This is more difficult with historical figures as we will
never know if they were transgender, homosexual or cross dressing
for other reasons. In historical references we have used the pronoun
the person was assigned at birth and then changed it when the
person transitioned. For other accounts, we have used the gender
pronoun that would have been used at the time they were alive.

Contents

Introduction

Today **transgender** is a big issue around the globe. There are trans celebrities, organisations for trans human rights, new rules and regulations supporting trans people in schools and at work and a lot of debate about what gender means and how it affects every one of us. **LGBTQ+** has become a universal name for the lesbian, gay, bisexual and **transgender** community.

Being transgender

Transgender refers to a person who feels their gender identity does not match the one given or assigned to them at birth. So a person assigned a female gender at birth might feel like a boy, or not feel like a boy or a girl (gender neutral) or sometimes feel like a boy and sometimes like a girl (gender fluid). Cisgender (cis for short) people are those who identify with the gender assigned to them at birth.

Two main words used here are gender and identity. Gender is not about sex. Gender is about how you dress, your name, how you behave and how your family, friends, community and culture may expect you to be. For example, if you're a girl people expect you to be feminine. Young girls wear skirts and dresses, have long hair and are expected to enjoy playing with dolls and prams. In some cultures females are expected to look after the home, to cook and clean and look after children and elderly parents. Males are usually expected to be masculine. Young boys don't wear dresses, have short hair and are expected to like to play with trains and cars. Generally an adult man is expected to be the 'breadwinner', the person who earns money to look after the family. Gender roles are changing around the world but there are still very strong expectations of how children and adults should behave depending on their assigned gender.

Identity is who we are, how we see ourselves, the sort of person we believe we are. Our identity is closely tied up with our gender, but also with our family and friends and our community. And our family, friends and community will see us in a certain way because of the gender we were given at birth.

In Mexico, the muxe community (see page 18) is a recognised third gender. They are boys and men who identify as women or who are gender neutral.

The third gender of Fa'afafine has been accepted in Samoan culture for generations (see pages 24–25).

What does this book cover?

Most of us accept that we are the gender we were assigned or given at birth — male or female — and live our lives accordingly. This is a binary or two-way lifestyle. In **Chapter 1** we look at many cultures around the world that have accepted a non-binary lifestyle for centuries. The families and communities of these cultures have accepted that some people live not as male or female, but identify as a third, fourth or even fifth gender, regardless of the body they were born with. These people express their different genders through the way they dress and behave and the roles they have in their community. They have their own history and social expectations and are part of myths and legends that go back hundreds of years.

In **Chapter 2** we explore how some individuals in the past lived in a non-binary or gender fluid way before 'transgender' was a label. They created a new identity for themselves based on gender. There is no way of knowing if these individuals were transgender, homosexual or just living life their own way, but their stories show how they achieved their preferred lifestyle by changing gender identity, for example women dressing as men so they could do work forbidden to women at the time.

TERMS

There are a lot of terms and labels used in the book. If you're not sure what words like 'gender fluid' and 'MTF' mean, don't forget to use the glossary on pages 60–61.

ALTERNATIVE PRONOUNS

A very important part of who you are is the pronouns you use to describe yourself. If you are not sure what pronoun to use when speaking to a trans person, ask politely — it is better to ask and get it right than use the wrong word. Mx is a gender neutral title often used instead of Mrs, Mr, Miss or Ms.

PRONOUNS

Male to female (MTF):	she	her	hers	herself
Female to male (FTM):	he	him	his	himself

GENDER FLUID/GENDERQUEER/GENDER NONBINARY/GENDER VARIANT:

	they	them	theirs	themselves
OR	ze	hir/zir	hirs/zirs	hirself/zirself

Chapters 3 and 4 look at how different countries react to the trans community and how trans people overcome huge obstacles to achieve their preferred way of living. Some countries have laws in place to help support the trans community, in other countries human rights are still a struggle for gay and trans people. In all countries the trans people want to be allowed to live the lifestyle they identify with, be it male, female, gender fluid or gender neutral.

Throughout the book, look out for the **Trans Now** panels which tell the stories of people from around the world who are currently facing the challenges of transitioning. Their inspiring stories help us to understand the issues facing transgender people globally today. ∎

Trans people overcome HUGE obstacles to ACHIEVE their preferred way of living.

This LGBTQ+ rally in North Carolina, USA, shows transgender flags (see page 9) and banners highlighting the issue of gender specific toilets. In March 2016 North Carolina passed a law that said only a person who has legally or surgically changed their gender can use the toilet facilities of their chosen gender.

Jake Graf and Hannah Winterbourne, both transgender, are patrons of one of world's first transgender charities, Mermaids. Jake and Hannah are married.

Jake, FTM

I knew from a very young age that I wasn't like other little girls. It wasn't that I wanted to play with cars and He-Man, wear trousers or call myself by a boy's name, it was something much deeper and unshakeable. My life as a girl was painful, humiliating and dark. I was bullied at school, tried to hide myself away from the world and effectively wasted many of my early years. I alienated my family, hurt many of the people I cared about and projected all of the anger and self loathing that I felt onto anyone I was close to. That said, friends and family stuck by me, and when I did eventually start to transition in my mid-20s it was with support, love and, finally, understanding.

Since my first shot of testosterone a decade ago I went from being someone with no prospects, mostly working in bars, to someone who now writes and directs award-winning films in what is a largely male-dominated industry.

As patrons of the Mermaids charity, working with trans children and their families, I see how important it is to support and love trans and gender nonconforming children from an early age, as it is only through showing them care and understanding that they will avoid a childhood

Jake Graf

"The tide is turning and the world is finally seeing that being transgender is not an abnormality but simply another part of the human condition..." Jake Graf

The transgender flag was created by trans woman, Monica Helmes, in 1999. The light blue stripes represent the traditional colour for boys; the pink stripes the traditional colour for girls. Both are overlapped by the white stripe in the middle. No matter which way up you fly the flag, it is always correct.

and youth full of self loathing, anger and sadness. The more role models those young folk have, the more hope there is for a positive future. The tide is turning and the world is finally seeing that being transgender is not an abnormality but simply another part of the human condition, and one that must be accepted without judgement.

What is becoming evident is that trans people have been around for centuries, in many guises: as trans men fighting for their countries, trans women living as famed artists and those more fluid and non binary folk present throughout history. Transgender is certainly not the trendy fad that the Press would have us believe.

Growing up as a young man in the 80s, I saw no representation of trans folk anywhere, positive or otherwise, and it made for a truly isolating, alienating and lonely childhood.

Now, I write stories about trans characters across history, in films that are screened around the world, in an attempt to broaden people's perceptions and understanding of the trans experience. It is absolutely vital that the trans communities around the world work together to make sure that the next generation of trans children grows up knowing that they are not alone, that there is nothing wrong with them, and that they too can be successful, happy and transgender. ■

Hannah, MTF

In my experience I have found 'gender' to be both very simple and very complex. Quite simply, my gender is female, and that is something that I have always known to be true, but I have also learned that gender is a spectrum, that it is a range of identities that are neither male nor female.

Having been assigned male at birth and subsequently transitioned to female, I have experienced life in both genders, which gives me a rather unusual insight into how society treats and interacts with men and women. Those differences tend to be subtle and often imperceptible to others but stand out to me. For example, I am an officer in the British Army, and I have the same respect and authority as a woman that I had as a man, but now I find that my colleagues swear less in front of me and that I am expected to be better at decorating for the Christmas party! However, I'm lucky to have had supportive family, friends and colleagues.

We now find ourselves at an interesting point in history where 'gender politics' are being discussed in all walks of life, and, for the first time, trans voices are being heard. We must take this opportunity to celebrate transgender people in all their diversity, showing the world that we are humans like everyone else. But we must also talk about inequality, discrimination and hatred against transgender people, and how far we still have to go. ■

Hannah Winterbourne

"We now find ourselves at an interesting point in history where 'gender politics' are being discussed in all walks of life, and for the first time trans voices are being heard. We must take this opportunity to celebrate transgender people in all their diversity ..." Hannah Winterbourne

Around the world transgender people are standing up for their rights and place in society.

1 Beyond Binary

In most western countries it is only recently that gender identity has been openly discussed as something that is not binary. But in many cultures around the world other non-binary genders have been recognised for hundreds of years.

Two-spirit people

Native Americans believe that people have an inner spirit that makes them the person they are, male or female. They believe that some people are gender variant, that is they have the spirit of both a male and a female. These two-spirit people are considered very special. In the past two-spirit people were often chosen to be spiritual leaders and teachers. Two-spirit people born as girls often became great warriors and hunters, which were traditionally male roles, and married women, while those born as boys would marry men and take the female role in the marriage, cooking, cleaning and weaving.

For many generations two-spirit people have been accepted and respected by many Native American cultures.

Two-spirit people prepare to dance, from the film *Two Spirits*.

Because two-spirit people had both masculine and feminine characteristics, they were considered hard workers, artistic and creative, and caring, and were respected and welcomed by their family and community.

Rejected by society

European settlers and Christian missionaries opposed the idea of two-spirit people and began the oppression of LGBTQ+ people. Marriages between two-spirit people were no longer recognised and two-spirit people were often rejected by society, abused and sometimes killed. Today the two-spirit population in North America is fighting for and regaining its rights and has a high profile at Pride marches and festivals. ■

A transgender beauty contest held in Mumbai every year helps trans women to gain acceptance and recognition (above and right).

Location:
India and
South Asia

The hijra

The hijra 'third gender' community in India, Bangladesh, Pakistan and other parts of Asia is thousands of years old. It traditionally refers mainly to those who were born male but lived their lives as women. Today the term refers to all intersex (see page 47) and transgender people. In past centuries the hijra community was an important part of Indian culture. The hijra were treated with respect and thought to be wise and spiritual. They are mentioned in India's great epic stories, the *Ramayana* and *Mahabharata*. However the hijra were turned into outcasts by the British when they colonised India in the 18th century. The British passed the Criminal Tribes Act of 1871, which outlawed the hijra community and attacked them for dancing and playing music and dressing as women. After years of abuse and living as outcasts, the hijra were finally recognised as a 'third gender' by the Indian government in 2014.

The British passed the Criminal Tribes Act of 1871, which outlawed the hijra community and attacked them for dancing and playing music and dressing as women.

But despite the 2014 legislation, hijras are still discriminated against, ridiculed, abandoned by their families and victims of police brutality. Many are forced to beg or earn a living as prostitutes. Some are paid to give fertility blessings, and dance at weddings and birth celebrations. Hijra communities often form on the outskirts of villages and towns where they can live together in some peace and safety, protected by a 'mother' or guru. ■

TRANS NOW:
NAINA, 18, MTF, INDIA

In 2015 at school assembly, when she was 16 years old, Naina told her whole school she was transgender. She was the youngest person in India to publicly declare her gender identity.

Since coming out Naina has put a video of herself online (see page 62) to help support the trans cause in India and started an online diary of her transition. Her openness helps many other young trans people around the world. She says she wants to start a 'conversation' to help break down barriers and increase understanding of LGBTQ+ issues.

One of the issues she now raises on her videos is the use of toilets at college:

"I can't go to the toilet if some young girls are using it; I have to use the nurse's loo. Why shouldn't I use the girls' toilet, I am a girl?" ■

Aravani of Tamil Nadu

In the southern Indian state of Tamil Nadu, the hijra are called Aravani. Like most hijra throughout Asia, the Aravani are treated as outcasts, discriminated against and harassed and abused. They form their own communities where they look after each other. For many the only way to make a living is to beg or become a sex worker.

At the annual Koovagam Festival, Aravani and other transgender people from around Asia gather to celebrate the story of Aravan (see below). It is also an opportunity to highlight the treatment of the trans community in Asia which is generally discriminated against.

This is a statue of the Hindu deity, Krishna, who could take male and female form.

The story of Krishna and Aravan

The Aravani community take their name from a story told in the Indian epic tale, the *Mahabharata*. The night before a battle the hero, Aravan, was told his army would win if they sacrificed a perfect male from among their tribe. Aravan, who was a virgin, offered himself on the condition that he spend one night as a married man, but no family was willing to offer their daughter as a bride when she would be widowed the next day. Finally, Lord Krishna took female form, married Aravan and spent a night with him. ■

Aravani art project

The Aravani Art Project is a group of Aravani that paint huge murals on street walls to raise awareness of the identity rights of the Aravani. They believe that art brings communities together: "The label of an artist can be transformative; it allows us to look at what people create and to understand one another beyond the labels we've given to our bodies and gender identities."

Indian transgender art

The Aravani Art Project is just one of several Indian transgender projects from across the arts, including poetry, dance and film-making. Some trans people are raising awareness of the trans community by working in high profile jobs such as radio and television. Their journey is often difficult. Shanthi Sonu turned her life around when she became a disc jockey for a radio station in Bangalore. In Hyderabad three trans women have started a YouTube channel dedicated to trans people to 'normalise' and support the trans community. ■

(Top) The Aravani Art Project paint a mural in collaboration with a local rap band called The Dawgz. The wall is a place where young people and children meet in Mumbai.

(Below) A mural in Bangalore. The writing says *Naavu Idhevi* — We Exist.

Location:
India

Muxes of Mexico

The town of Juchitán, in the southern state of Oaxaca in Mexico, is home to a group of third gender people called muxes (pronounced MOO-shay). Some muxes are identified as men at birth but believe they are really women and live their lives as women, others live a non-binary lifestyle. The muxes are accepted by the local Zapotec community and are generally considered a blessing by their families. Muxes often fulfill traditional female roles such as looking after elderly parents, helping around the house or making and selling handicrafts to bring in extra money. Mothers are usually pleased to have a child who is muxe to help with the cooking and cleaning. Female family and friends often help muxes to dress and behave as women, however muxes cover the whole spectrum of gender identity.

Muxes often fulfill traditional female roles such as looking after elderly parents, helping around the house or making and selling handicrafts to bring in extra money.

A muxe (sitting), with friends in Juchitán, Oaxaca state, Mexico.

In November a four-day festival, the Vela de las Intrepidas (loosely translated this means 'celebration for those that like to live dangerously'), is a huge party to celebrate the lives of the muxes. Thousands of partygoers turn up from around Mexico and the world. ■

Muxes dress up in glamorous dresses and traditional costume to celebrate at the Vela de las Intrepidas.

Location:
Mexico

BEYOND BINARY

5 genders, Indonesia

The Bugis people of Sulawesi in Indonesia recognise not two or three genders, but five. They are females, males, calalai (females that live as men), calabai (males that live as women) and bissu, who are hermaphrodites or intersex. Because bissu have the characteristics of both male and female, it is believed that they have special powers and are able to communicate with the spirit world. Bissu are often asked to perform ceremonies to bless people, for example to ask the spirits for safety on a long journey.

Above left: a bissu is preparing for an initiation ceremony for another bissu.

Above right: a trans woman helps a young bissu bride prepare for her wedding.

Calalai and calabai are not considered transgender as they have no desire to change their body by taking hormones or having surgery. They are happy in the body they have but dress, live and behave as the opposite gender.

The Bugi believe that the calalai, calabai and bissu are essential to a balanced and harmonious society. ∎

Location:
Indonesia

Because bissu have the characteristics of both male and female, it is believed that they have special powers and are able to communicate with the spirit world.

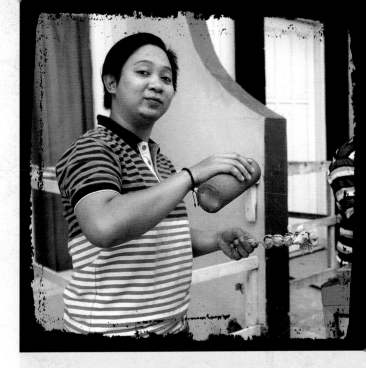

Above: JK identifies as a calalai, a trans man. Although calalai don't have a specific role in Buginese society they are accepted as part of the community.

Below: Wanda, left, has cut her hair and wears men's clothes even though she still identifies as a woman and is called Wanda by her family.

Mahu, Hawaii and Tahiti

In Hawaii and Tahiti mahu is the name given to people who are not male or female, but both or neither ... a middle gender. Traditionally they were special people treated with great respect and totally accepted by society, but in the 18th century western countries started to invade Hawaii and forced their own religious beliefs on the islanders. The mahu were banned as being an abomination to the Christian God. The people were repressed and forced to accept western religious beliefs and the mahu became outcasts. Today the mahu are slowly being accepted back into society again, but they still face discrimination in schools, jobs and housing. ■

King Kamehameha I of Hawaii (c. 1758–1819) had mahus dwell near his house because he considered them lucky, and in Tahiti every village had one mahu because this was thought to bring luck to the village.

Locations:

Hawaii

Tahiti

These mahu from Hawaii (right) and Tahiti (left) are considered to have both male and female characteristics.

Fa'afafine, Polynesia

In Samoa, a Polynesian island, boys and girls are expected to behave in ways associated with their gender. For example, girls help with the housework and look after the elderly while boys go out to work. In families that have all boys, it is accepted that parents raise one or more of the boys as girls to help with the household chores. The boys are dressed as girls and taught the tasks that girls would do, such as cooking, sewing and handicrafts. These boys who are brought up as girls are called Fa'afafine, which means 'in the way of women'. The boys are not always transgender, but accept the role the family give them.

As they grow older and even once they marry (to a woman), Fa'afafine may continue to dress as women and do women's work. Having women's skills and the strength of a male makes Fa'afafine valuable members of the community. Today some boys have a difficult time accepting the role of Fa'afafine when they want to live as males, while other boys choose to be raised as Fa'afafine.

Today, many third gender communities around the world have to fight for their human and civil rights. They are battling against religious prejudice, intolerance and ignorance. ∎

Location:
Samoa, Polynesia

Left and right: Fa'afafine individuals often say they believed they were girls as children, but as adults realised they were men who choose to live as women. In Samoan society children are not expected to conform to strict binary gender roles as many children in western cultures are.

Location:
Northern
Ireland

There have always been individuals who have ignored **gender expectations**. Were these people transgender as we know it today? It is impossible to know as gender issues were either unknown or just becoming recognised. We do know that they chose to dress, behave and live in a way that went against society's expectations for their **assigned birth gender**. Their reasons for doing this vary but all their stories are extraordinary and brave.

From Margaret to James
Dr James Barry (c.1795–1865),
Surgeon

One of the most extraordinary and innovative surgeons of his time, Dr James Barry became a fully qualified surgeon on 2 July 1813 and joined the British Army on 6 July. During his life-long career in the army he was posted to South Africa, Mauritius, the West Indies, Corfu, Malta and Canada. He transformed hospitals wherever he was posted by improving sanitation, diet and medical care for all, including the poor, lepers, prisoners and slaves. He never married and no long-term relationships have been recorded, but he adored animals and always travelled with a pet dog. When he died in 1865, it was discovered that the much admired and highly respected Dr Barry was actually a woman.

Dr James Barry (left) with John, a servant, and his dog, Psyche.

Dr James Barry, born Margaret Bulkley in Northern Ireland, wanted to be a doctor, a profession considered unsuitable for women in the 19th century. He studied medicine at Edinburgh University, living life as a man because women were not allowed to enrol in medical schools at this time. ■

It is believed Dr Barry dressed and lived as a man in order to attend medical college and become a surgeon.

TRANS NOW:
MICHAEL, 15, FTM, UK

Michael would often watch guys on TV and feel jealous that they were able to live as men. He knew that trans people existed, but believed they were freaks and he felt too normal to be a freak.

Aged 12 Michael started to wonder whether he might actually be a guy. A few weeks later Michael began to come out to his friends, who overall were accepting. But his parents would not accept it. Eventually Michael couldn't bear pretending to be a girl anymore and talked to his school about transitioning. He started wearing a boy's uniform aged 14. His friends stood next to him while he made the announcement to his year group.

The reaction was mixed. A lot of people called him names behind his back. A few teachers were transphobic too. However his situation has improved since he first came out. His parents still aren't supportive, but they tolerate it and Michael has become much more confident since transitioning. ■

Pine Leaf (1806–1858), Native American Warrior

Pine Leaf (left and below) was a member of the Gros Ventres or White Clay tribe, who lived in the area now known as Montana, USA. Pine Leaf was kidnapped by the Crow tribe when she was ten years old. Some stories say that the leader of the Crow tribe wanted to raise Pine Leaf as a young male warrior to replace a son he had lost, others that Pine Leaf herself wanted to learn the skills of a boy. Whatever the reason, Pine Leaf was raised as a male and taught traditional male fighting and hunting skills.

Many believe that Pine Leaf was a two-spirit person (see pages 12–13). She thrived as a young 'male' warrior and her hunting and battle skills and bravery were legendary, but she always dressed as a woman. She was later given the title Woman Chief and was war chief of her tribe until her death. She had four wives, led her army into many successful battles and held high office among the tribal chiefs. She eventually negotiated a peace with the Gros Ventres tribe, but was ambushed and murdered by a Gros Ventres party. ■

Location:
USA

From Marguerite to John
Radclyffe Hall (1880–1943)
author

Marguerite Radclyffe Hall (above, right) was the only child of a demanding, bullying, selfish mother, and a father who abandoned them both. She was born in Bournemouth, a seaside resort in England. She lived a life of emotional and physical turmoil as a child and was dyslexic, but her family was wealthy and had lots of artistic connections. Marguerite soon learned that music helped her dyslexia and she also enjoyed writing.

It became clear to Marguerite that she was attracted to women. As soon as she was old enough she left home with the money she had inherited on the death of her father, and began to live as she wanted. She cut her hair short and wore it slicked back, dressed in tailored suits, cravats and bow ties, and called herself John. Today we do not know whether Radclyffe Hall would have identified as trans or a cross-dressing lesbian.

Radclyffe Hall developed a career as a writer, publishing poetry and novels. She made headline news with her novel, *The Well of Loneliness* (1928), a story about lesbian love. A British magistrate said the book encouraged people to recognise and accept lesbianism and was 'obscene', and ruled that all copies be burnt and the book banned. This ruling was reversed after her death and the book was published again in the UK in 1949. Today the book is generally regarded as a turning point in homosexual literature. ∎

Location:
England, UK

From Einar to Lili

Einar Wegener (1882–1931), Artist
(the Danish Girl)

Einar was born in Denmark and was assigned male at birth. He studied art in Copenhagen and married another young painter, Gerda, when he was 22 and she was 19. Gerda was a fashion magazine illustrator and began to ask Einar to model women's fashions for her portraits. Einar realised that being a woman was his preferred self and that it felt wrong behaving and living as a man. Einar and Gerda travelled in France and Italy for a while and settled in Paris in 1912, when Einar started to live his life more and more as a woman. He would dress as a woman to attend balls and outings with Gerda and resume his male role at home. His identity issues caused him to have a near nervous breakdown and he saw several psychiatrists who treated him for mental illness, subjecting him to painful, brutal and humiliating treatments for the insane.

Einar's female identity was called Lili. Einar loved being Lili and eventually told Gerda that Lili was the person she wanted to be and that she wanted to live the rest of his life as a woman. She never changed back. In the 1920s Lili travelled to the Clinic for Sexual Science in Berlin, Germany where Dr Magnus Hirschfeld was pioneering sexual reassignment surgery. The surgery meant Einar could legally change her identity to Lili on her passport. Lili chose the surname Elbe after the River Elbe that runs through the city of Dresden. Lili was now officially the person she longed to be ... Lili Elbe. Lili decided to have one more operation that she hoped would allow her to have children, but shortly afterwards she died of complications from the surgery. ∎

In the 1920s Lili travelled to the German Clinic for Sexual Science in Berlin where Dr Magnus Hirschfeld was pioneering sexual reassignment surgery.

Location:
Denmark

From Marion to Joe

Joe Carstairs (1900—1993),
Speedboat racer

Marion Carstairs (above, right) never accepted the fact that she was a girl and never behaved in a way expected of a young girl of her time. She was a boisterous, wild tomboy whose main interest was boats. Born in London to a wealthy American family, she was sent to boarding school aged 11 where she excelled in sport and spent her pocket money buying boys' pyjamas and shoes. When she left school Marion went to Paris to live with her divorced mother. She soon found herself part of a lesbian circle that included wealthy and glamorous literary figures.

During the First World War (1914—18) Marion worked as an ambulance driver in France and Ireland and loved it. Many women at this time discovered that they had the strength, spirit and ambition to live a different sort of life. These women were no longer satisfied by the roles society gave women at this time and wanted more from life.

After the war Marion inherited a lot of money from her family. She bought expensive cars and raced around the countryside in them. She also began her lifelong passion for speedboats and speedboat racing. With a boat building company on the Isle of Wight she developed the fastest speedboats possible. Marion had long since cut her hair short, wore tailored clothes, had tattoos, exercised to keep fit and muscular and had the nickname 'Joe'.

Joe was an excellent and fearless speedboat racer who adored the thrill of speed. Joe entered male-only speedboat races (there were no female racers at this time) where she was accepted as one of the 'men'.

In 1934 Joe bought Whale Cay Island in the Bahamas. It was a wealthy island but Joe built a lighthouse, a power station, a school and a museum, as well as a Spanish villa-style house for herself where she threw huge and riotous parties. When she became elderly, she left the island and went to Florida, USA where she died. Joe lived a long, eventful and unconventional life that suited her male identity. ■

From Dorothy to Billy

Billy Tipton (1914–1989),
Jazz musician

Born in Oklahoma City, USA, Dorothy's parents divorced when she was four years old. She and her younger brother went to live with their Aunt Bess in Kansas City where Dorothy learnt to play the piano and saxophone. Dorothy was a big, awkward girl, and never really seemed comfortable in the kind of feminine dresses other girls wore.

In 1933, aged 18, Dorothy graduated from high school, passing all her music exams, and headed back to Oklahoma to live with her mother. She wanted to play in a jazz band but touring bands didn't employ women at that time. When she heard of a band looking for a saxophonist, she hatched a plan. She bound her chest with a piece of old sheet, cut and slicked back her hair, put on a man's suit and got the job! Her family was appalled at the cross-dressing so Dorothy broke all ties with her aunt and father and was free to develop her male persona. Billy Tipton (sitting at the piano, below) was born.

Billy had at least two wives and lived with other women. He told them he'd had a serious car accident when he was younger that had damaged his genitals. He claimed he had to keep his chest bound with elastic bandages to help support his ribs as a result of the accident. The women who shared his life had no idea that Billy was a woman. He adopted three boys and was always known to them as 'Dad'. But when he visited his mother, Billy became Dorothy again.

No one really knows why.

Professionally, Billy enjoyed great success in the 1950s with his own jazz band but died in poverty aged 74. He collapsed in a trailer park van and the medics who came to treat him opened his pyjamas to feel for a heartbeat and discovered his secret. Billy died without regaining consciousness. ∎

She bound her chest with a piece of old sheet, cut and slicked back her hair, put on a man's suit and got the job!

Location:
USA

TRANS NOW:
SEBASTIAN, 17, FTM, USA

Sebastian was assigned female at birth and called Erika. When he was little he hated his ponytail and dresses. Erika was born in Mexico but moved to Bethlehem in the USA in his teens. At his new school Erika was introduced to Sasha, a trans MTF student. Sasha had found a clinic that gave hormone therapy and helped explain to Erika about being transgender. This was Erika's first introduction to transgender. Up until then she thought she was a tomboy lesbian.

Erika was lucky. At the Mazzoni Center in Philadelphia she received hormone treatment even though she was under the age of 18 and needed financial help to pay for the treatment. About a year after starting treatment Erika went to school and announced that he had a new name, Sebastian. The hormone treatment also increased his self-esteem and he was now able to pass more as a male, consequently felt happier about his appearance.

Overall Sebastian had a lot of support from his teachers and classmates. But he recalls one teacher who was dividing the class into boys and girls and forced him to go with the girls, even though his classmates stood up for him and said he should go with the boys. Sebastian says this made him feel 'uncomfortable, angry and sad'. ∎

From George to Christine
Christine Jorgensen (1926–1989),
entertainer, transgender campaigner

Christine was the first person to make the American public aware of transgender issues. Born George Jorgensen and growing up in the Bronx, New York City, USA, George hated wearing boy's clothes and wanted to be like his sister. As a young man George was quiet and shy and attracted to men, but never felt that he was a homosexual. George felt like a woman in the wrong body, and was 'lost between the sexes'.

George came across an article about Dr Christian Hamburger who was experimenting with gender therapy in Denmark, so in 1950 George headed for Denmark to meet Dr Hamburger. He immediately recognised that George was a transsexual and encouraged him to start living as a woman and to begin hormone treatment. George felt that at last someone understood what he was suffering and didn't think he was just mad. After a year of hormone therapy and evaluation by a psychologist, George began to have sexual reassignment surgery. The lessons learnt from the pioneering surgeries performed on Lili Elbe (see page 30) may well have helped to make the surgery a success.

After the surgery she wrote to her parents, 'Nature made a mistake which I have had corrected, and now I am your daughter.' Her parents were very supportive.

"Nature made a mistake which I have had corrected, and now I am your daughter."

Christine Jorgensen

George returned to the USA as Christine (named in honour of her surgeon), a slim, blonde female. The US papers made her headline news. She was offered film and stage work, toured as a singer and did media interviews about her transition, helping to raise awareness of gender dysphoria. She was never able to marry because at that time her birth certificate could not legally be changed from male. ∎

From Richard to Renée
Renée Richards (1934–),
tennis player

Richard Raskind was the son of a wealthy family from New York, USA. She trained to be an eye surgeon and joined the Navy as a physician where she pursued her love of tennis, winning all the Navy tennis championships. Richard appeared to have the perfect life — but she was tormented by the life-long belief that she had been born into the wrong body.

As a child Richard dressed in her sister's clothes and as an adult secretly dressed as a woman at home, shaved her legs and tried to disguise her genitals. She had extensive psychiatric help, started hormone therapy and even lived as a woman for six months in Paris. Richard chose the name Renée, which means 'reborn'. But Renée decided to give life as a man one more go, got married and had a son. The marriage fell apart three years later and Renée was reborn, but this time she was here to stay.

Richard appeared to have the perfect life – but she was tormented by her life-long belief that she had been born into the wrong body.

Renée transitioned officially in the 1970s and decided to play in women's amateur tennis tournaments. Thanks to a newspaper story, it soon became public knowledge that Renée had been born a man. The tennis world was split. The United States Tennis Association barred her from playing professionally, claiming she had an unfair advantage in terms of strength, and while some female players supported her, others also claimed her birth as a male gave her unfair advantages in a women's game. However in 1977 the New York Supreme Court ruled that Renée Richards was female and therefore could play in women's tennis tournaments. Renée continued to play for a few years before retiring from tennis, having left a legacy that is a huge victory for the transgender community. ■

An unfair advantage?

Many believe that in some sports trans women have an advantage over cis women. Some experts claim that bone and muscle strength is stronger in MTFs especially if they have been through puberty. Today many doctors and specialists say that hormones, especially testosterone, can affect strength and ability, and that MTF should wait for a year after taking hormone replacement therapy before being allowed to compete in women's competitions. However different sporting organisations around the world have different opinions. Many trans athletes globally still have a hard time being accepted in professional sporting competitions. ■

3 – Power People

Location:
Australia

Today, in many countries and professions around the world, **openly transgender** people are taking positions of authority and power. This helps to increase recognition and acceptance of the trans community. For most of the people whose stories appear in this chapter, transitioning and coming out was incredibly brave. Their decision to do so raises the profile of transgenderism and begins to help its acceptance in their own country and often in the wider, international community. It also sets examples to other countries and gives support and inspiration to other trans people.

Australia

Bridget Clinch is aiming to become the first Australian trans politician. She was assigned male at birth and, after completing high school, joined the Australian Defence Force (ADF). After being in the ADF for about II years and completing two overseas deployments, Bridget told her chain of command that she needed to transition. ADF policy at the time stated that people undergoing sex reassignment treatment were not suitable for service because 'of the need for ongoing treatment and/or the presence of a psychiatric disorder'. Bridget fought against this policy, arguing that the UK and Canadian militaries both allowed trans members to transition and continue to serve for many years. Eventually the policy was cancelled and trans members were allowed to transition and keep serving in the armed forces.

"My career ended, and I'm still suffering from the depression and anxiety that came from the conflict and breakdown in the relationship between me and the army that I served." Bridget Clinch

This progress was not without controversy in Australia. Many objected to trans treatment being covered by the ADF, however ADF medical policy at the time covered any and all evidence-based treatment needed to keep its members fit, healthy and ready to deploy on operational service. Bridget has noted that many ADF people were supportive, but that most of the opposition she faced was from people higher up in the chain of command in Canberra. In 2017 she said:

"My career ended, and I'm still suffering from the depression and anxiety that came from the conflict and breakdown in the relationship between me and the army that I served."

In 2018 Bridget Clinch was shortlisted for the Australian LGBTI Awards. These are awarded to people who have helped to raise the issues surrounding the LGBTI community.

A few years after Bridget fought to enable trans people to serve in the Australian military, US President Donald Trump tweeted that transgender troops will be banned from the US military, encouraging conservative politicians in Australia to speak out about trans military service. Bridget was published and quoted in the media talking about how this undermined the progress made for trans rights.

Bridget is a member of The Greens (a political party) and has run as a candidate in a state and a federal election. She hopes to run again in future for federal parliament or the senate. She hopes that her open and honest approach to politics could get her elected where she can continue to push for progress and rights for all.

In the same year, US President Donald Trump's tweets saying that transgender troops will be banned from the US army encouraged conservative politicians to say it should be the same for Australia, but at that time Bridget's courageous stand has enabled other trans troops to remain in the army.

Bridget is now standing for parliament for Brisbane's Veteran's Party. Brisbane is the capital of Queensland, traditionally a very conservative state. When Bridget joined the Veteran's Party many members left in protest, but other party members believe in her policies and trust that her open and honest approach will help raise the profile of the party and could lead to her becoming the first trans politician in Australia. ∎

The Australian government has pushed for greater diversity in recruitment for the ADF. It has support services for LGBTQ+ members.

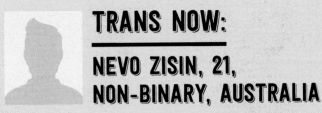

TRANS NOW:

NEVO ZISIN, 21, NON-BINARY, AUSTRALIA

Nevo Zisin was assigned female at birth but by the time Nevo was at nursery school, Nevo would only wear boys' clothes and wanted to be accepted as a boy. Now Nevo identifies as non-binary and prefers the pronouns they/them. Nevo lives in Melbourne in Australia and is from a Jewish family. Nevo spent a year learning how to behave like a 'good' Jewish girl in order to take part in the traditional Jewish coming-of-age ceremony for girls, bat mitzvah. Nevo felt unsure about their sexuality and gender identity and eventually came out as a lesbian aged 14.

Nevo went to the first Australian Jewish school to join the Safe Schools Coalition (see page 63) and they say the support they received because of this saved their life. Nevo had suicidal thoughts and depression and thought that life might have gone in a very different and very negative direction if they hadn't been at a safe school.

Nevo's gender dysphoria worsened and Nevo came out as transgender in the last year of high school. Nevo's family is important to them and the family were at the centre of Nevo's decision to finally transition to male at the age of 17. Nevo works as a youth leader and takes workshops and runs gender identity programs in schools.

In 2017 Nevo published *Finding Nevo,* an autobiography.

"I hope fellow trans people will feel less alone, heard and seen. I hope they realise that there is a future for them and that they are strong and resilient. I hope cis people read this book and feel a responsibility to create safer spaces and a safer world at large for trans people. In general, I hope this book will inspire people to create change, both within themselves and in society." Nevo Zisin ∎

"I hope fellow trans people will feel less alone, heard and seen. I hope they realise that there is a future for them and that they are strong and resilient." Nevo Zisin

Location:
China

China

Jin Xing was assigned male at birth but grew up wanting to be feminine like her sister. When she was nine she joined the People's Liberation Army performance troupe, hoping to channel her inner girl. Training was hard and painful but in 1986, aged 18, Jin won a national dance competition.

Two years later she travelled to New York on a scholarship to study modern dance. This led Jin Xing to perform and teach dance in Europe. During this time she felt she might be gay, but then had the sudden realisation, "a weird feeling in myself — that I should be a woman" and she eventually returned to China to have gender reassignment surgery. Chinese doctors had no experience of such operations but Jin says she wanted the surgery in China because: "I need the chi, I need the earth... to protect me. In a Western environment maybe the technology is there, but my soul is too lonely."

Jin Xing formed her own dance company, the Jin Xing Dance Theatre, and performed around the world as the leading female dancer.

During this time she felt she might be **GAY**, but then had the sudden **REALISATION**, "a weird feeling in myself — that I should be a **WOMAN**".

When Jin Xing had the surgery in 1985, homosexuality was still considered a crime in China, and was classified as a mental disorder. Jin, however, was fully supported by her parents. In 2000 she adopted three Chinese orphans and soon after married a German man. In 1997 homosexuality was decriminalised in China and in 2001 it was struck off the mental disorder list. But the LGBTQ+ community in China still faces discrimination, bans on public meetings, a lack of legal rights, and LGBTQ+ couples cannot marry or adopt children. There are strict legal guidelines for gender reassignment surgery that include being over 21, unmarried and having parental consent which is usually difficult to get. ■

In 1997 homosexuality was decriminalised in China and in 2001 it was struck off the mental disorder list.

TRANS NOW:

ALEX, 35, FTM, RUSSIA

Life is difficult for trans people in Russia. They have no legal or police protection. There are few medical professionals who have the knowledge to help transgender people. Many trans people become outcasts, suffer terrible violence and verbal abuse, are discriminated against, can't get jobs or benefits, are abandoned by friends and family and live in poverty. Suicide rates are high. Alex is one of the lucky ones.

Aged 21, Alex obtained a certificate from a psychiatric hospital in Moscow that said he had a condition called 'transsexualism'. This is a legal requirement to allow trans people to start transitioning. Alex was allowed to change his passport and other legal documents from female to male, and he began hormone treatment. However he lived in a small city and couldn't get a job. Eventually a friend helped to pay for him to go to St Petersburg, a big city in Russia, to have gender reassignment surgery. Alex still lives in Russia but says he's afraid to go out at night. He just wants to live a normal life, unafraid. ∎

In Eastern Europe organised parades help to raise the profile of the LGBTQ+ community and their rights.

India

Gopi Shankar Madurai is one of the youngest and first openly intersex and genderqueer candidates in the Legislative Assembly of the Tamil Nadu region of India. Gopi uses the pronouns ze and hir. Since ze was a teenager Gopi has fought for intersex and trans rights. Hir has set up organisations to fight against injustice, attended world conferences and helped many trans and genderqueer women escape forced prostitution and sex work.

When Gopi started to campaign as a candidate for the Legislative Assembly hir received many death threats and was sexually and verbally abused. Gopi's position helps raise the profile of genderqueer people in a positive way, and means hir can fight for their future legal protection. ■

Gopi Shankar Madurai represented Hinduism and the LGBTQIA+ community at the World Pride Madrid in 2017, one of the biggest LGBTQIA+ events, which is supported by the United Nations and the European Parliament.

Locations:

Germany

India

Germany

Balian Buschbaum was a young athlete affected by his decision to transition. As Yvonne Buschbaum he was a successful pole vaulter but had to give up the sport when, aged 27, he decided to begin the treatment to transition into a male. This was because the hormones he would have to take to change his body were banned for athletes.

Today Balian is a life coach, fitness trainer, nutritional expert and motivational speaker. His positive lifestyle and success as a businessman help encourage other trans people and prove that anything is possible, regardless of your background. His message is that whether you are straight or LGBTQ+, being healthy, honest and communicating with one another is a good way to live. ■

Balian Buschbaum on the German television show, 'Let's Dance'.

What is intersex?

Unlike most transgender people who are assigned a gender at birth, intersex/ VSC (variations of sex characteristics) people are born with a mix of both male and female biological characteristics such as male and female genitals, chromosomes and sex hormones. Being intersex is not a disease, an illness, a deformity or a disorder, the body just varies a little from what is generally considered to be a 'typical' male or female body. However in many cultures intersex/VSC babies are abandoned or even killed at birth, and can be discriminated against and made an outcast by their community.

In western cultures, parents of intersex babies or doctors have the right to assign a gender to the child that includes surgery and hormone treatments given to the child to 'correct' the imbalance and to make the child a binary-accepted male or female. The majority of intersex/VSC babies have one sex that is stronger than the other so in the majority of cases surgery and other treatments are not needed. Treatment can also cause chronic pain, incontinence, loss of sensation and mental issues throughout life. The right of intersex people to choose their own gender has now become a human rights issue supported by the United Nations. ■

"The first thing you get used to when you put on a police uniform is getting judged by your appearance and stared at on the street. It's not dissimilar to being transgender."

Rhona Stace

New Zealand

Sergeant Rhona Stace is one of the first transsexuals to work for the New Zealand police, but for 20 years she was known as Constable Rohan Stace, a husband and father of two, trying to ignore her true identity. Then, in 2013, Rohan began to transition to a woman. She learnt about make-up from a friend and watched fashion shows on TV to pick up advice on how to dress. Although Rhona was excited to live her preferred life, she still had suicidal feelings and "pretty serious demons still lurking around in my head". A year before she fully transitioned she divorced her wife, but told her children she would always be their 'dad'.

Rhona accepts that there is a grieving process when someone transitions. Close family and friends can feel that they have lost a person they love and have to get used to a new person. Rhona had a lot of support and acceptance from the police, but thinks that 20 years ago it might not have been so positive. She says being a cop helped her to transition:

"The first thing you get used to when you put on a police uniform is getting judged by your appearance and stared at on the street. It's not dissimilar to being transgender."

As a man, Rhona says she was very aware of 'boy stuff' and 'girl stuff' and rigidly did the 'boy stuff' because she was afraid of being outed. Today she paints her fingernails glittering gold and wears high heels to court. ∎

"I have been through unpleasant situations when I have met people who have shown contempt or displeasure. Because I am very well-recognised in Poland now, it gives me a lot of opportunity to observe reactions to me, and there are a lot more postive reactions than negative reactions." Anna Grodzka

Anna Grodzka, centre, marching with the Polish group at Gay Pride in London in 2012.

Poland

When Anna Grodzka was elected to power in the Polish parliament in 2013, she was the world's only transgender MP. She became involved in politics as a student and continued in politics while developing a career in film and publishing. Married with a son, she realised she was transgender when she was in her 20s, but because of her marriage continued to present herself to the outside world as a man.

Anna finally made the decision to live her life as a woman in 2007. Telling her family and friends was very hard and her wife and many friends snubbed her. Poland is a deeply Roman Catholic country and the Church has a huge influence on the politics of the country. LGBTQ+ issues are not tolerated, although Anna believes this is changing, helped by her high-profile position in office. ∎

Location:
Poland

Peru

In 2014 Luisa Revilla became the first openly trans person to become a politician in Peru. This is a huge achievement. The Roman Catholic Church, which is traditionally anti-gay, still has a strong hold on the politics and culture of Peru, where homophobia and transphobia is rife. Peruvian law does not ban discrimination against the LGBTQ+ community. As a result, the LGBTQ+ community still faces poverty, police brutality and lack of job opportunities, forcing many to turn to lower paid jobs and prostitution. ■

Luisa Revilla

A Pride march in 2017 to promote acceptance and tolerance of the LGBTQ+ community in Peru.

"I am going to promote equality and I will say no to discrimination. We want everyone to have equal access, to succeed and to achieve their goals." Luisa Revilla

Location:
Peru

Uruguay

In October 2017 Michelle Suárez became the first openly transgender person to be elected to the senate in Uruguay. She is also the first trans woman to graduate from a university and to be a lawyer in the country. The law in Uruguay allows same-sex marriages and adoptions, and people can legally change their gender without undergoing surgery. However Michelle wants to take this even further and establish laws that allow trans people to legally change their gender without a court order and to set aside one per cent of government jobs for trans people. ■

Location:

Uruguay

Michelle Suárez (centre) realised she was a transgender female when she was 15. She says her parents have always supported her but some teachers and classmates discriminated against her and it was a 'tough time'.

"We have to talk about the rights of couples and families, about the gender identity act, about the mutilation of intersex children, and about discrimination, which includes hate crimes, bullying, workplace harassment and access to housing and healthcare." Tamara Adrian

Venezuela

A lawyer and LGBTQ+ rights activist, Tamara Adrian was the first transgender politician to be elected to the National Assembly in Venezuela in 2015. Before becoming a politician Tamara worked as a lawyer and LGBTQ+ activist. Tamara had gender reassignment surgery in 2002, but had to register as a member of the Assembly under her given name of Thomas Adrian as the law in Venezuela does not allow anyone who was assigned male at birth to change to a female name or identity. ∎

Tamara Adrian (right) is a big supporter of the World OUTGames, a 10-day event hosted by the gay community for all people, regardless of sexual orientation or gender identity. She believes sport is a great way to unite people of all cultures and backgrounds.

TRANS NOW:

MANDISA, 20, MTF, SOUTH AFRICA

It was hard for Mandisa growing up with no one understanding her and seeing her as a delinquent. She had no one to support her and was abused because she was transgender. She started cross-dressing at 19 and was amazed at how beautiful she had become. A lot of people could not tell she was a man but there were always some people pointing fingers. Mandisa still has a long way to go. She wants to finish her degree next year and then start hormone treatment, but she doesn't know how she will be able to afford it. Mandisa is optimistic about the future but finds life very hard. ■

TRANS NOW:

TUSHEBA, 22, MTF, UGANDA

Since childhood, Tusheba has always felt like a girl. In her late teens she began to dress in a more feminine way and changed her hair. Her family said she was a curse on them. Tusheba came from a poor family and did not have enough money for school fees. Now living as a transexual, she was introduced to sex work by a friend while she was living in a hostel. She was able to earn enough to pay fees to attend a language school to learn English and survive. However, she was thrown out of clubs and pubs because she was a transwoman and suffered physical violence and harassment, including being burned with cigarettes. She was harassed by the police, including a time when the police undressed her, took her bag, money and phone, and cut her hair. However, when her father became very ill, she was able to pay his hospital bills using the money earnt from sex work. It was because of this that her father forgave her and accepted her as a trans woman, though she was still rejected by the rest of the family. ■

Location:
USA

USA As well as transitioning herself, Dr Marci Bowers has helped pioneer sexual reassignment surgery and is considered one of the finest gender reassignment surgeons in the world. Assigned male at birth, Dr Bowers tried to transition aged 19 but failed because she didn't have the support from her family or the funds to pay for treatment. She married and had three children, but has since had surgery and completed the transition from male to female. She remains married to her wife and says they are 'closer than sisters'. Dr Bowers has helped advance the acceptance, safety and quality of sex reassignment surgeries. She also does FGM (female genital mutilation) reversals, often free of charge, and campaigns against FGM. ∎

"Transitioning is like walking on lily pads: You have to be careful with each step, or you're going to sink. It takes a lot of money, courage and a certain amount of planning. I'm just glad I can help."

Marci Bowers

Marci Bowers says: "Binaries are not natural, especially when it comes to gender." She believes being transgender "doesn't need to be as scary as it used to be, so don't be afraid".

"These past six years, people have seen me as a woman,

not a transsexual. People in the gym, people I train with,

it's been great, it's been awesome. I'm just a woman to them.

I don't want that to go away. It's unfortunate that it has to."

Fallon Fox

USA Fallon Fox (right) was assigned male at birth and named Boyd Burton, but from a young age felt different. In 2006 Fallon went to Thailand to get the surgery she needed to become the women she knew she really was and came back to the US as Fallon Fox. She became a professional MMA (mixed martial arts) fighter but kept her transition secret. When she was outed by a newspaper reporter the secret sent shockwaves through the sporting world and opened up an ongoing controversy about trans people taking part in professional sports. Fallon was angry that the sporting world saw her only as a trans woman and not a female athlete. She said in a 2013 interview: "These past six years, people have seen me as a woman, not a transsexual. People in the gym, people I train with, it's been great, it's been awesome. I'm just a woman to them. I don't want that to go away. It's unfortunate that it has to."

Some people said Fallon's success as an MMA fighter was down to her being born into a male body rather than because of her skill. She argued that having been on hormone therapy for 10 years and having had gender reassignment surgery any advantage she might have had was long gone. Along with other transgender athletes and sportspeople, Fallon fought against being labelled as a trans female athlete. She just wanted to be accepted as a female athlete. She has now retired from the sport. ■

USA Recently trans black people have been making a huge impact in local politics in the USA. In November 2017 Andrea Jenkins was the first openly trans female of colour to win a seat in public office in the USA. She was elected to the Minneapolis City Council, Ward 8.

Andrea Jenkins has helped another trans person achieve political success. She organised a Minnesota Trans Equity Summit to encourage trans people to apply for positions on boards and committees in Minneapolis. Here she met Phillipe Cunningham, a young, black, gay trans man.

Before moving to Minnesota, Phillipe was a special needs teacher in Chicago. He didn't tell any of his colleagues at the school where he taught that he was trans. He found the work environment 'hostile' and 'transphobic' and says he struggled because he was effeminate and shy. "I found myself isolated in my workplace. I was mocked and ridiculed. I became the butt of everyone's jokes." He also experienced racial prejudice. Eventually, "There came a point when I knew it was time to leave the classroom to make a larger impact and have the freedom to bring my authentic self to my work."

Phillipe moved to Minnesota and began a new career as a youth public policy adviser. Thanks to the trans equality policy Andrea Jenkins was promoting, Phillipe eventually stood for election in the 2017 local election in Ward 4 in Minneapolis, and won. ∎

"… as an African-American trans-identified woman, I know first hand the feeling of being marginalised, left out, thrown under the bus. Those days are over. We don't just want a seat at the table, we want to set the table."

Andrea Jenkins

Phillipe Cunningham and Andrea Jenkins

"Just because some people may not know how special you are, doesn't mean you are not special," Phillipe Cunningham

TRANS NOW:
SARAH, MTF, IRAN AND CANADA

As a child growing up in the late 1980s in Tehran, Sarah was uncomfortable wearing the clothes and playing the games expected of boys and felt she didn't belong at an all-boy's school. When she reached puberty life got worse. She had to deal with sexual harassment from her classmates and was called names. Her life as a teenager was 'total hell'.

Because of government censorship, trans issues are not openly discussed in Iran and the Internet is censored, so Sarah couldn't research transgender or discuss how she felt with others. Sarah realised she was trans when she was in her early 20s. She told her family and a few close friends but had to hide it from everyone else. She then had to decide whether to have gender reassignment surgery.

"On the one hand I really wanted to do that and be free and liberated from all the problems of my past. On the other hand I was so scared ... because I thought I [would] lose everyone and everything that I had fought for. My university degree, my job, everything. I saw myself having to stand against the entire world."

Sarah decided to undergo the gender reassignment surgery but had to save up for six years to pay for it. During this time she dressed and lived as a man and managed to get a job. She had the surgeries in Thailand when she was 28.

After the operations Iranian law allowed Sarah to have her gender changed on her legal documents such as her passport. But life is not so easy for many trans people in Iran. They suffer from verbal abuse and discrimination. Sarah now lives and works as a journalist in Canada but has helped to set up a trans rights organisation in Iran. ■

Timeline

Around the world, for decades, people have been fighting for trans rights. These are just a few of their major achievements.

1930 Einar Wegener travelled to Germany to undergo experimental gender reassignment surgery to become a woman, Lili Elbe.

1951 Roberta Cowell was the first UK transsexual to undergo complete sex reassignment surgery.

1952 Christine Jorgensen (born George William Jorgensen in 1926) was the first trans woman to become well-known in the USA.

1969 Trans women riot with others at Stonewall, USA, in what is now seen as the start of the modern LGBTQ+ movement.

1972 Sweden was the first country to allow people to legally have gender reassignment.

1977 The New York Supreme Court allows MTF Renée Richards the right to play professional tennis as a woman.

1980 The American Psychiatric Society used the term 'gender identity disorder' for transgender people.

1995 Georgina Beyer was the first openly transsexual mayor in the world, elected to office in Carterton, New Zealand.

1998 Dana International was the first transsexual woman to win the Eurovision Song Contest for Israel with a song called 'Diva'.

1999 The first International Transgender Day of Remembrance was held on November 20th. It was started by Gwendolyne Ann Smith, a trans woman, in memory of the murder of trans woman Rita Hester in Massachusetts, USA. Today it highlights the violence and discrimination transgender people face every day around the world and is celebrated in nearly 200 countries. It comes at the end of Transgender Awareness Week.

1999 Georgina Beyer was elected as the world's first openly transsexual member of parliament in New Zealand.

2004 Sarah Lurajud (MTF) became New Zealand's first openly transsexual police officer.

In Thailand the first Miss International Queen beauty contest took place and has become the biggest beauty show for transgender women in the world.

2007 In Nepal, the Supreme Court ordered the government to recognise a legal third gender category based on a person's 'self-feeling' rather than medical or legal authority.

2008 The world's first national human rights report on discrimination against transgender people was published. It was called 'To Be Who I Am' and was commissioned in New Zealand.

2011 In Australia the government passed legislation that allowed passports to include a third gender option.

2012 Argentina passed a law that allowed anyone over the age of 18 to choose their own gender identity, have gender reassignment surgery and revise official documents to their referred gender without any medical or legal ruling. Children could do so with their parent's consent or that of a judge. This is seen as a huge victory for trans human rights and it is hoped other countries will follow.

2014 Legislation in India gave people the legal right to identify as a third gender and gave them legal protection. However discrimination against the LGBTQ+ communities in India is still rife.

2015 Germany was the first European country to allow parents to leave the gender blank on the birth certificate if their baby is born intersex (see page 47). This is to allow the child to decide its own gender identity when old enough.

RTÉ Irish radio station host, Jonathan Rachel Clynch, came out as gender fluid at work with the support of the radio station's management and colleagues.

The International Olympic Committee (IOC) passed guidelines that stated that trans people could compete without having had sex reassignment surgery, as was the case previously. The IOC stated that trans women had to wait a year after starting hormone treatment before they could compete, to allow hormone levels to stabilise.

2016 It is believed that Sara Kelly Keenan was the first person in the USA to receive an intersex (see page 47) birth certificate. Sara was identified as male when she was first born, but after a few weeks her birth certificate was changed to female. Now, aged 55, she has been given a new birth certificate that gives her sex as intersex.

2017 In China a court ruled that a man was unlawfully fired from his job because of his gender identity, a huge victory in a country that is notoriously homophobic.

The Methodist Church ordained its first transgender minister, MTF Joy, in Kent, England. She married and lived as a man until coming out as transgender.

The State Sports Council of Kerala, India, organised the world's first state-level sports meeting for transexuals. Over 100 athletes turned up. Many said they didn't have the opportunity to do sport at school because of discrimination, bullying and lack of facilities for trans people.

2018 The World Health Organisation is due to release a revised version of the International Classification of Diseases which will change the way medical professions around the world treat trans people, for example, taking transgender-related issues out of the mental disorders section.

Glossary

bat mitzvah a Jewish religious ceremony for 12-year-old girls to celebrate becoming an adult

binary a system of two; refers to the traditional gender system of male and female

chi in Eastern medicine a form of energy that is essential for a balanced and healthy body and mind

cis short for **cisgender**, a term given to people who are the gender they were assigned at birth (male or female) and not transgender

colonised when people from one country take over and govern the people of another place

conservative holding traditional values; not liking change

conversion therapy treatment that was believed to cure patients of homosexuality in countries and societies where homosexuality was considered a mental illness that could be 'cured'

cravat a short wide strip of fabric worn around the neck by men. It was tucked inside the shirt

decriminalised when the law or government says that something that was a crime is no longer a crime, such as homosexuality

discriminate to treat someone unfairly because of their age, sex, colour, religion or gender

epic tale a long story full of heroes, usually based on mythological characters

FGM stands for female genital mutilation and is when part or all of the outside of the female genitals are cut away. It is extremely dangerous and painful and is illegal in most western countries

FTM stands for female to male

gender dysphoria a medical term to describe the unhappiness and conflict felt by those who do not feel comfortable with their biological sex

gender fluid a mixed gender identity which can vary over time

gender identity how a person sees their identity as a male, female, both or neither

gender nonbinary not identifying as either male or female

gender reassignment surgery when a person has surgery to make their body more like their preferred identity, such as removing breasts in FTM

genderqueer people who do not identify with traditional gender definitions such as male or female but may feel a combination of both or neither

gender variant people whose gender behaviour or expression does not match the gender they were assigned at birth

guru traditionally a Hindu religious and spiritual leader and teacher; often a knowledgeable, experienced older person who guides and advises others

hermaphrodite having both male and female sex organs and other sexual characteristics

hir a pronoun used by people who are gender fluid instead of him or her

homophobia a hatred or fear of homosexuals; prejudice and discrimination towards homosexuals

homosexual a person who is attracted to people of the same sex

hormones a chemical substance produced by the body to help it grow and work properly. During puberty the body releases hormones that develop the body to become fully male or female

hormone treatment/therapy using hormones as a medical treatment to make the body develop more female or male characteristics

human rights a basic way of life including free speech, safety and equality that are the rights of every individual on the planet regardless of age, sex, colour, religion, race or class

intersex/vsc (variations of sex characteristics) people who are born with genitals or other sexual characteristics that are a mix of male and female

leper a person suffering from leprosy, an infectious disease that affects the skin and nerves

lesbian a woman who finds other women sexually attractive and is not attracted to men

LGBTQ+ stands for lesbian, gay, bisexual, transgender, questioning, plus. Can also include I for intersex and A for asexual

The Mahabharata an epic Sanskrit story from ancient India

misgendered to use a word such as a name or a pronoun that does not match the gender identity of the person, for example to call a MTF, Mr

missionaries a person who travelled overseas on a mission to convert people to Christianity

MTF stands for male to female

nervous breakdown a period of mental illness as a result of depression, stress or anxiety

nymph a beautiful maiden in mythology, usually living in rivers or woods

outed when someone's sexual preferences or identity has been revealed against their wishes

prostitution when people are paid for having sex

Ramayana an epic poem about Prince Rama and his wife Sita, from ancient India

ridicule to make fun of, mock, a form of verbal abuse

sanitation the removal of toilet waste and dirty water; providing a clean and healthy environment for the community

senate a part of the government in certain countries such as the USA and France

sexual reassignment surgery (SRS) a series of surgical operations to change a person's genitals and remove breasts for a FTM so that their body resembles their preferred identity

testosterone the hormone that helps develop male characteristics

third gender a name given to a group of people who identify as neither male nor female

transgenderism when a person's preferred identity does not match the one given at birth

transition to change from one gender to another

transphobia a hatred and fear of transgender people

transsexual a person who has changed the gender given to them at birth

two-spirit a Native American whose body expresses both feminine and masculine spirits

virgin someone who has never had full sexual intercourse

ze a pronoun used by some gender fluid, gender nonbinary, gender varient or genderqueer people to replace him/her and he/she

For More Information

Websites and videos

- A support resource for students and carers/parents based in Australia: *www.safeschoolscoalition.org.au/*

- Find out about the human rights issues of the LGBTQ+ communities around the world: *www.hrw.org/topic/lgbt-rights*

- An organisation that promotes respect and value for all members of the school community. Education resources for teachers and schools as well as ideas for how students can create a more inclusive school environment: *https://www.glsen.org/gsa*

- A National Geographic video on the Bugis 5 Genders: *www.bing.com/videos/search?q=Indosnesian+%25+genders+video&view*

- Listen to an interview with Bridget Clinch in Australia: *www.youtube.com/watch?v=qBL1GCQ9MuQ*

- The human rights of transgender people in Europe: *www.weforum.org/agenda/2016/05/this-is-what...*

- Read an interview with Phillipe Cunningham: *www.advocate.com/commentary/2015/09/08/op-ed-black-gay-trans-man-minneapolis-city-hall*

- US trans teenagers — stories and video: *http://mashable.com/2015/08/31/transgender-teenagers/#qcH1SEtblgqK*

- What its like to be transgender in Russia: *https://themoscowtimes.com/news/russias-transgender-community-struggles-for-acceptance-video-49411*

- A visual roundup of LGBTQ+ rights around the world: *http://infographicworld.com/lgbt-rights-around-world/*

- Interview with Naina (p15): *www.youtube.com/watch?v=sZMI2oPE2qM*

Books

- *The Queen of Whale Cay* by Kate Summerscale, Fourth Estate 1997. A biography of 'Joe' Carstairs.

- *Suits Me. The Double Life of Billy Tipton* by Diane Wood Middlebrook, Virago Press, 1999 About the double life of Billy Tipton.

- *The Trials of Radclyffe Hall* by Diana Souhami, Virago Press, 1999 An insight into the life of Radclyffe Hall.

- *The Secret Life of Dr James Barry* by Rachel Holmes, Tempus Publishing , 2007. A biography of Dr James Barry.

- *Some Assembly Required* by Arin Andrews, Simon & Schuster, 2014. Arin's story of how he transitioned from female to male.

- *Rethinking Normal* by Katie Rain, Simon & Schuster, 2014. Katie's journey from being a boy to being a girl.

- *Can I tell you about gender diversity?* by C J Atkinson, Jessica Kingsley Publishers, 2017. An introduction to transgender and transitioning for trans people, their friends and family.

- *Beyond Magenta: Transgender Teens Speak Out* by Susan Kuklin, Walker Books, 2016. Interviews with six transgender and gender neutral young people about their trans journey.

Helplines

If you need advice, check out a website or call a helpline and talk to someone who will understand.

For readers in the United Kingdom

- *http://gids.nhs.uk/young-people* The Gender Identity Development Service is part of the Tavistock and Portman Clinic. It advises and counsels families and young people on gender issues. Read the stories of some young people who've been to GIDS.

- *www.childline.org.uk*
  Find out about issues that are troubling you, meet others, message or call the 24-hour helpline for advice or talk to someone who'll just listen. *Helpline: 0800 1111.*

- *http://genderedintelligence.co.uk*
  Free downloadable pdfs, school visits, creative workshops, activities and groups to bring trans young people together. Online forums, residential weekends and advice and support for young trans people by trans people.

- *www.mermaidsuk.org.uk*
  Advice, counselling, and support for young trans people and their families. Online separate teens and parents forum. School training supplied. *Helpline: 0844 334 0550* (charged); mobile only: *0344 334 0550.*

- *www.nhs.uk/conditions/Gender-dysphoria*
  Explains gender dysphoria, has video real-life stories and further useful links.

- *www.sandyford.org*
  NHS service in Scotland

- *www.samaritans.org*
  Advice and support for anyone in distress. The helpline is *08457 90 90 90.*

- *www.supportline.org.uk*
  A charity giving emotional support to children and young people.

For readers in Australia and New Zealand

- *www.transcendsupport.com.au*
  Online support network and information hub for transgender children and their families. Helpline on *1800 55 1800.* Or Lifeline on *13 11 14.*

- *www.trucolours.org.au*
  Counselling, information, videos, support groups, education services and much more for the transgender community.

- *www.changelingaspects.com/LinksPages/Support%20Groups.htm*
  A list of transgender support groups in Australia and New Zealand.

- *www.healthdirect.gov.au/partners/kids-helpline*
  A helpline for young people giving advice, counselling and support.

- *https://kidshelpline.com.au*
  Online and phone help for a wide range of issues.

- *www.kidsline.org.nz*
  Helpline run by specially trained young volunteers to help kids and teens deal with troubling issues and problems.

- *www.studentwellbeinghub.edu.au/*
  Part of the Safe Schools Coalition Australia (SSCA) to provide information and resources for the wellbeing of the whole school community including students, teachers, parents and carers.

For readers in the United States and Canada

- *www.openarmsproject.org*
  Aims to bring together LGBTQ+ youth to end isolation and build a supportive and empowering community.

- *www.transequality.org*
  The National Center of Transgender Equality supports social justice for the trans community, discusses trans rights, gives support against discrimination and has a blog.

- *www.thetrevorproject.org*
  A 24/7 helpline for the LGBTQ+ community. Call *1-866-488-7386*, text or message.

- *www.glbtnationalhelpcenter.org*
  Youth hotline: *1-800-246-7743*
  email: *help@LGBThotline.org*
  LGBT National Help Center gives online support plus chat lines and talk groups:

- *https://thelifelinecanada.ca/lgbtq*
  An online resource with loads of information:

Global

- A list of crisis hotlines around the world:
  https://thelifelinecanada.ca/help/crisis-centres/international-crisis-centres/

  https://liamrcarter.wordpress.com/2015/09/05/list-of-lgbt-friendly-helplines-worldwide/

Index